W9-BXD-100

extending
forgiveness

extending forgiveness

VIRGINIA H. PEARCE

DESERET
BOOK

Salt Lake City, Utah

Visit us at DeseretBook.com

Library of Congress Cataloging-in-Publication Data

(CIP data on file)
ISBN 978-1-60907-714-3

Printed in the United States of America
R. R. Donnelley, Crawfordsville, IN

10   9   8   7   6   5   4   3   2   1

The Lord has endless ways of teaching us what He wants us to know. Not infrequently in my personal scripture study a theme will float to the top. I find myself noticing all sorts of passages on the same subject. And then I start hearing talks about that very subject everywhere I go, or I notice articles on it in the *Ensign,* or I hearing people discussing the topic. Does the Lord sometimes teach you that way too?

Several months ago, I was with a friend, telling her about a particular topic that seemed to be on my mind for no apparent reason. She said to me, "Well, maybe it's what the Lord wants you to speak about at Time Out for Women this year."

I have heard a million talks about the fact that we should forgive. I've heard all kinds of messages about how important it is to forgive others, and that we should just do it. My challenge, as I began to go through the scriptures and search my heart—and particularly as I went off on my own quest for forgiveness, the one the Lord wanted me to take—was that I didn't know very many "hows."

I said: "Well, maybe it is. It's an odd thing, but I am just fascinated by this, and everywhere I go, I seem to be hearing stories that have to do with this principle."

The conversation went on, drifting to one thing and another as we spent the evening together. Somewhere along the way she mentioned a mutual friend, telling me how hurt this friend had been by another friend's behavior. I found myself talking about how hurt *I* had been by this same woman, ya-da, ya-da. . . . As I drove home that night, I started to feel really bad about what I'd said. I immediately called my friend and said, "I am so sorry I said that."

She said, "And, Virginia, you were wondering why the Lord wanted you to learn about *forgiveness?* Perhaps He is trying to teach you something . . ."

She was right. I have heard a million talks about the fact that we should forgive. I've heard all kinds of messages about how important it is to forgive others, and that we should just do it. My challenge, as I began to go through the scriptures and search my heart—and particularly as I went off on my own quest for forgiveness, the one the Lord wanted me to take—was that I didn't know very many "hows." I wanted to forgive but I didn't know what to do.

> I wanted to forgive but I didn't know what to do.

I am not going to give you a tidy list of "what to do first, second, or third." What I *am* going to do is share with you a few of the scores of stories I have been collecting about forgiveness. I hope they'll give us some clues that will be helpful to you—as they were helpful to me—about *how* to go about extending forgiveness.

The first story is about a woman who found herself sitting in the reception room of a lawyer's office several years ago. She was consumed with hate. She'd been wronged by a man, and she was here to make him pay. She wanted to do to him what he had done to her. She wanted to take from him his money, his energy, his time, and, most of all, his façade. She wanted him to suffer as he had made her suffer. And she knew, as she was sitting there, that the law was on her side.

She later reported that as she was waiting in the lawyer's office, she was preparing a Church assignment. She had a lesson to give the following Sunday, and she was reading from the New Testament, making notes and outlining her thoughts, when she came upon this passage from Ephesians: "And be ye kind one to another, tenderhearted, forgiving one another, even as God for Christ's sake hath forgiven you" (Ephesians 4:32).

She later described her reaction to the words: "I can never verbalize the spiritual power of that message to my heart. It was as if all the teachings of the gospel came together into one great whole, and in that instant I could see through a glass clearly rather than 'through a glass, darkly'" (1 Corinthians 13:12). She continued to report: "My feelings for this man did not change. What he had done to me did not change, but I changed. In that moment of instant awareness, I felt for the first time in my life that the Savior could save *me*."

The story didn't end there, however. Things continued to get worse. The man in question became intent on making her life as miserable as possible. It got to the point where even her health was practically ruined. She had pneumonia, she couldn't function, and it seemed like everything was failing.

One day, in the course of a conversation, her mother said, "We *will* forgive him." It was another reminder of a truth that would become more than just a statement. It would be a long journey, but my friend kept forgiveness as the goal. It was in her prayers as well as her scripture reading. She looked up every scripture in the Topical Guide under the heading of *Forgiveness.* She read them each many, many times until they slowly began to make sense in her world, helping her to know what her responsibility was and what the Savior's responsibility is. She enlisted the support of her amazing parents, who

$\mathcal{M}$y feelings for this man did not change. What he had done to me did not change, but I changed. In that moment of instant awareness, I felt for the first time in my life that THE SAVIOR COULD SAVE ME.

would listen to her for hours on end and always help her focus on her goal to forgive.

One day, three years later, she was walking down the street when suddenly a feeling of lightness came over her. And the words that came to her mind were the words that she had wanted to say for three years but hadn't been able to. At that moment, she said them out loud. She said, "I forgive him." Remember, it took three years for her to get to that point, but at last she was able to say, "I forgive him."

What's more, that feeling has lasted. It has been many years, but she reports, "Even now, sometimes when I go to the temple, I put his name on the prayer roll, asking the Lord to bless him that good things will happen in his life."

That's forgiveness, isn't it? That's the kind of forgiveness we all want to have the strength and the insight to be able to extend.

Let's just look at that story for a minute and identify some of the things it teaches us about the process of forgiveness. I believe one thing we learn is that sometimes forgiveness is instant, but sometimes it takes time. However long it may take, though, having the *desire* to forgive, making forgiveness our goal, is our burden. This is how we exercise our agency in the whole process: we keep forgiveness as the goal, even if we can't forgive right away.

Sometimes forgiveness is instant, but sometimes it takes time.

My friend's story also says to me that forgiveness is possible even when there is no restitution, no remorse on the part of the perpetrator. She never had a conversation with him about what he had done to her. He never said he was sorry. And yet she was still able to forgive him. That suggests to me that forgiveness is not between me and the one who has hurt me; it is between me and the Lord.

Let me repeat that principle: Forgiveness isn't just between two people. First and foremost, it's between you and the Lord. Why would that be? Think

Forgiveness

is not between me and the one who has hurt me; it is between me and the Lord.

about it. Think about the fact that the Savior came to earth in order to forgive everyone's sins. When He did that, He paid for the sins of the people who have hurt us, didn't He? So our holding out against those people and trying to punish them is really taking upon ourselves something that isn't our job. We don't have the right to revenge. We don't have the right to hold that person's feet to the fire. That judgment belongs to the Savior because of what He did for all of us. That is part of His mission.

Consider the fact that the person we have really offended when we can't extend forgiveness to those who have wounded us is the Lord. That's the relationship that is ruptured, and it's a far greater sin to separate ourselves from the Lord than it is to rupture the relationship between two human beings.

We are mortals. And, as such, we make mistakes. Nobody goes through life without inflicting some damage unintentionally on other people. And the closer those people are to us, the more possibility of damage. I could probably make a list of how I have hurt each of my children, for example. And I'm certain my children could make their own lists of how they have been damaged by me, and those lists probably wouldn't even match!

We all create pain for others, however unintentional it might be. When a new baby is placed in our arms, we vow to love, nurture, and protect that child. But, sadly, we are all mortal beings, and very often the greatest wounds we inflict are those we have no idea that we are inflicting. So each of us needs to learn how to seek and how to extend forgiveness.

Speaking of the wounds, who heals our wounds? Is it the people we've had the conflicts with? Although it's nice if they say they are sorry and want to make it up to us, they can't really heal our wounds, can they? That's also the Savior's job—to bind up our wounds. He does the forgiving, and He does the binding up. So once again, we see that the whole struggle to extend forgiveness is really between us and the Lord. This further demonstrates the importance of desire in the process.

President Gordon B. Hinckley said, "If there be any . . . who nurture in their hearts the poisonous brew of enmity toward another, I plead with you to ask the Lord for strength to forgive." That's our part of the equation, isn't it—to go to the Lord and ask Him for strength to forgive. President Hinckley continued, "This expression of desire will be of the very substance of your repentance" ("Of You It Is Required," 62).

> Consider the fact that the person we have really offended when we can't extend forgiveness to those who have wounded us is the Lord.

Do you see what he is saying? Somebody wounds us, and we think he or she is the person who needs to repent. But when we withhold our forgiveness from that person, then *we* are the ones who have to repent. I don't know why it's so hard to want to do it, to find that desire in our hearts. Could it be that if I give up my enmity, if I give up my hatred, if

Sadly,

WE ARE ALL MORTAL BEINGS, AND
very often the greatest wounds
we inflict are those we have no
idea that we are inflicting.

SO EACH OF US NEEDS TO LEARN
HOW TO SEEK AND HOW TO EXTEND
FORGIVENESS.

I give up my bad feelings, then the person who hurt me gets off scot-free? I can't have that happen!

That's ridiculous, isn't it? There is no such thing as getting off scot-free in the Lord's economy. That will all be taken care of with the Lord.

President Hinckley said further of forgiveness: "It may not be easy, and it may not come quickly. But if you will seek it with sincerity and cultivate it, it *will* come. . . . There will come into your heart a peace otherwise unattainable" ("'Of You It Is Required,'" 62).

Think about my friend and her three-year struggle to seek and cultivate forgiveness. Didn't you just love that when she had the kind of peace President Hinckley speaks of, there was a lightness all of a sudden that she recognized? I love the phrase in Isaiah that identifies the Messiah as one who will offer "the garment of praise for the spirit of heaviness" (Isaiah 61:3). That's what I heard my friend saying: that she got "the garment of praise" in return for giving up "the spirit of heaviness." And that's the exchange we make when we experience the miracle of forgiving someone who has wronged us.

President James E. Faust said, "Most of us need time to work through pain and loss." He told of "a sister who had been through a painful divorce" and "received some sound advice from her bishop." Her bishop said, "Keep a place in your heart for forgiveness, and when it comes, welcome it in" ("Healing Power of Forgiveness," 68). I like that image: "Keep a place in your heart for forgiveness, and when it comes, welcome it in." It may not be tomorrow; it may not be in three years; it may take longer, but keep that place in your heart and welcome forgiveness in when it comes.

One more thing we can learn about forgiveness from my friend's story is that we will know our forgiveness is complete when we have a genuine desire for the welfare of the people who have wronged us. It's not when we just quit thinking about what they did to us; it's when we have a desire for their welfare. When my friend put that man's name on the prayer

"Keep a place in your heart for

FORGIVENESS,

and when it comes,

welcome it in."

rolls of the temple, in an expression of her desire for his welfare, it was an indication to *her* that her forgiveness of him was complete. I love that.

The next story I'd like to discuss to illustrate some principles about forgiveness is from the scriptures. It is the story of a man in the Book of Mormon who is one of my favorite people: Pahoran. In this account, the Nephites are under siege from the Lamanites. Lamanite forces are invading the land; they are taking cities. The capital city of the Nephites is Zarahemla, and Pahoran is the chief judge, in other words, the head of the government in Zarahemla. Captain Moroni is out in the field with the troops, trying to retake some of the cities that have been captured by these bloodthirsty Lamanites. Helaman is doing the same thing in another area. War is being waged on several fronts. And the reinforcements don't come, and the armies are short on food, and the slaughter ensues, and so Moroni writes a letter to Pahoran that, honestly, is the meanest letter I have ever read in my whole life.

Moroni accuses Pahoran of holding out and not sending reinforcements or food. "And now behold, I say unto you that myself, and also my men, and also Helaman and his men, have suffered exceedingly great sufferings; yea, even hunger, thirst, and fatigue, and all manner of afflictions of every kind.

> We will know our forgiveness is complete when we have a genuine desire for the welfare of the people who have wronged us.

But behold, were this all we had suffered we would not murmur nor complain. But behold, great has been the slaughter among our people" (Alma 60:3–5). Moroni basically unloads everything he has suffered, and then he says, "Can you think to sit upon your thrones in a state of thoughtless stupor, while your enemies are spreading the work of death around you?" (Alma 60:7).

Have you ever received a letter that was that mean? I have not. Of course, Moroni is a good writer, and that helps get his point over, but he goes on, page after page.

"But why should I say much concerning this matter? For we know not but what ye yourselves are seeking for authority. We know not but what ye are also traitors to your country" (Alma 60:18). So not only does Moroni accuse Pahoran of being in a thoughtless stupor, he accuses him of being a traitor. On and on and on. He finally tells Pahoran that if he doesn't get it together, Moroni will see personally that he is punished.

Well, it turns out that, unknown to Moroni, Pahoran has been deposed by some traitors in Zarahemla, so he is unable to do anything, but somehow he gets this lovely letter. And this is his response: "Behold, I say unto you, Moroni, that I do not joy in your great afflictions, yea, it grieves my soul" (Alma 61:2). He goes on: "And now, in your epistle you have censured me, but it mattereth not; I am not angry, but do rejoice in the greatness of your heart. I, Pahoran, do not seek for power, save only to retain my judgment-seat that I may preserve the rights and the liberty of my people" (Alma 61:9). Pahoran expresses love for Moroni all through his epistle, telling him how much he admires his great heart. Finally he says, in effect, "I was so glad to receive this letter because I didn't know what to do, and now we can make a plan together to defeat our enemies." And that is what they do.

A forgiving nature—I don't think that happened to Pahoran overnight. I think that takes years and years of practice. One of the important things I notice in this story is his absolute refusal to be offended. Is that part of forgiveness, that we simply refuse to be offended in the first place? Pahoran is able to avoid feeling offended because he looks behind the offense to the intent. He says, in essence, "I know you have a great heart and you only care about the people, and I feel the same way about the people." One of the things we can think about when we are trying to extend forgiveness to somebody is, *What was the real intent?*

Is that part of forgiveness, that
we simply refuse to be offended
in the first place? Pahoran is
able to avoid feeling offended
because he looks behind the
offense to the intent.

I don't think most of us mean to hurt other people. By and large, we are trying to make something work, either for ourselves or for somebody else, and we are blind to what we are doing. We don't get up in the morning and say: "Boy, I sure hope I can ruin somebody's life today, and I hope it's one of my kids or my husband. Let's get up there and get going, and let's wound them; let's make them bleed." We don't do that, do we? Our intentions are generally good, but we often hurt people inadvertently, and we get hurt by others in the same unintentional way. So part of being forgiving is to go back and try to understand what the other person's motives really were. If we do that, I think most of the time we'll find that the motives were good, it was just the action itself that hurt us.

> Part of being forgiving is to go back and try to understand what the other person's motives really were.

Another story about forgiveness features a good Christian woman who was a physician, as was her husband—in fact, they worked in the same office for many years. They had some children. And then he had an affair with one of the nurses. The wife was absolutely eaten up by heartbreak and bitterness. She prayed, but she could get no relief.

Then one day, she decided to sit down and write him a letter. She thanked him in every specific way she could for everything that he had given her. She talked about his good qualities that had blessed her life. And as she finished the letter and mailed it, that longed-for release happened. She forgave him. Isn't that an interesting thing?

I think gratitude has to be one of those principles that is part of forgiveness. Gratitude flips the switch that allows us to forgive because it allows us to see the good. In this case, the husband had a history of years and years of good things he had done for his wife. She lost it all when he became unfaithful to her, but those good things really did happen, didn't they?

Gratitude flips the switch that allows us to forgive because it allows us to SEE THE GOOD.

And as she expressed her gratitude for them, the heaviness lifted. "Beauty for ashes, . . . the garment of praise for the spirit of heaviness" (Isaiah 61:3).

Another woman came from a rural life where her father was a rancher, and he could do everything; he could fix everything; he could make everything work. She went away to school and fell in love with a man who could not have been more the opposite of her father. He knew whole operas by heart; he loved nothing more than to go to symphonies and art museums, and she loved that about him. She fell in love with him, and they married. They lived in a large city and took part in all of the arts. But as the years went by, she began to focus on the things that he didn't do—you know, when he couldn't fix things in the house, when he couldn't keep the place running like her father had done so effortlessly. In public, she made jokes about him; she put him down in front of their children; she complained to her friends; she expressed irritation at every point until that was all she saw in him. The marriage ended in divorce. She simply could not forgive him for being himself.

Think about that for a minute. None of us can be everything to everybody. We all have to let those around us have a chance to forgive us for being ourselves.

Holding on to expectations is often the source of unforgiving feelings, isn't it? We sometimes hold on to "this is what a husband should be," "this is what a child should be," "this is what a best friend should do for me," "this is what grandparents owe their grandchildren." Our expectations about the way people should behave create unforgiving feelings, and with those unforgiving feelings we start to shut our hearts off so that we can't feel love for those people, we can't feel their love for us, and we certainly can't feel the Lord's love for us in the same way we had before.

We would do well to remember that none of us is who the Lord wants us to be—not yet. Think about His expectations for us. Is He unforgiving because we don't meet them yet? He's giving us time, isn't He? He grants us the time and space to grow and forgives us along the way as we fall short.

Many of us carry scars from adolescence. It's a time of insecurity when the actions and words of our peers can burn holes in our hearts. As the years go by, we generally forget about these feelings, but once in a while, when a name comes up, we find ourselves struggling again.

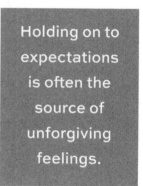

Holding on to expectations is often the source of unforgiving feelings.

That's exactly what happened to my husband, Jim. He felt he had been misused by an acquaintance during those tender years and, as time went by, an unforgiving spot in his heart just kind of solidified. It didn't mean much; he hardly ever thought of it, in fact.

Fast-forward decades. The offending person became a prominent figure in the community. His name appeared sometimes in the newspapers, and

None of us can be EVERYTHING to everybody.

We all have to let those around us
have a chance to forgive us for being

when Jim saw this, I glimpsed the struggle in his heart. He said: "I have to get rid of this. I know in my head that this isn't the same person. That was fifty years ago. I've changed; he's changed." I noticed him working to listen to the good things others said about this man. I sensed his struggle to extend forgiveness and am quite certain that he was asking for help from the Lord.

> Those hard feelings, all those emotional burdens, had been lifted.

Then Jim was diagnosed with a terminal illness. And one day this man, with whom we had had very little contact over the years, called on the telephone and asked if he could come for a visit. He'd heard that Jim was sick and wanted to see him. Jim didn't say anything to me about it other than: "So-and-so called and wants to come over this afternoon."

A short time later, the doorbell rang. I opened the door and invited him in. Then I sat in the living room and listened to the two men talk. It was the sweetest experience. Neither one of them talked about their early years; they didn't even mention the incidents that they probably both remembered. But they didn't need to. There was no elephant in the room that day. It was absolutely sweet. The friend had brought a gift. He'd remembered some things about Jim that had guided him in choosing that gift. They chatted pleasantly for a while, and then, just before the man left, Jim said to him, "Would you be willing to give me a blessing?"

This man laid his hands on Jim's head and gave him the most loving and powerful blessing imaginable. And then they shook hands and embraced one another, and he left. As I shut the door behind him, I realized it was gone. Those hard feelings, all those emotional burdens, had been lifted.

This is the miracle of the Atonement. This is what Christ can do that we cannot do on our own. I know Jim had tried to forgive that man on his own. I don't know at what point he turned to the

Lord and asked for help, but I am confident that's what happened—that his desire and his prayer to be strengthened by the Lord to be able to forgive had resulted in the granting of that miracle. I don't know what the other man had done, but I do know that forgiveness is not only possible, it is the sweetest thing we can experience in this life. And it's no wonder that the Lord has absolutely commanded us to repent and forgive one another. It's not optional— not if we want to come back into His presence. It is part of our receiving the Atonement. It is what we must do.

President James E. Faust said, "We need to recognize and acknowledge angry feelings." I'm grateful to know that forgiveness doesn't mean we have to pretend someone didn't hurt us. We acknowledge our pain, but then, President Faust taught, we need to "get on our knees and ask Heavenly Father for a feeling of forgiveness" ("Healing Power of Forgiveness," 69). When we have been hurt, slighted, or wounded unfairly, we are not left alone to bear it. We can get on our knees and ask for the Lord's help to forgive.

Elder Neal A. Maxwell said: "Some of us let the past lock us in, rigidly refusing to reclassify other people, which can be devastating to the development of anyone. We must permit others to press forward too" (*Wherefore, Ye Must Press Forward*, 91). We know that we have grown and changed with the years. We must let other people move on as well and not insist on keeping them where they were before.

Forgiveness is not only possible, it is the sweetest thing we can experience in this life.

We always have a choice when we are wounded. We can retaliate, attempting to return the pain to the one who inflicted it. We can pass the hurt on to someone else. Or we can metabolize the pain and treat others differently than we've been treated. Christ is the supreme example of taking the pain in and then not passing it on, instead metabolizing it and diffusing it. We mirror God's mercy to us when we forgive another. To wait upon the Lord, whether it is fifty years or three years or ten minutes, means to trust Him and to believe that in time He will help us. We need to trust that when we are truly ready to forgive, He will facilitate it.

I believe that if there is one place we need forgiveness, it is within our families. I love this statement about families that appears in a textbook used at Brigham Young University: "Without the kind of forgiveness that stems from the Atonement—that pays the demands of justice and fully heals all family members—there is no eternal family." Think about that. We're not just talking about the "I'm sorry" moments; we need the power of the Atonement to satisfy justice and to heal our wounds. Without that forgiveness, our families cannot last eternally, for "living families petrify and hearts turn to stone under the gradually accumulating layers of hurt and pain over the years. The Atonement of Christ redeems us individually and redeems our

What is better than to lay down the burden of pain, to be healed by His love, and to then be free to extend that same love to those who have hurt us?

relationships" (Harper and Butler, "Repentance, Forgiveness, and Progression," 155).

I believe that. I believe if we let things build up and are unforgiving in our families and homes, our families will petrify and harden. On the other hand, if we create a forgiving family—if we forgive others and allow them to forgive us—we use the Atonement more fully in our lives.

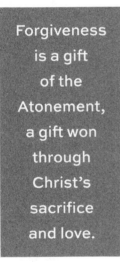

Forgiveness is a gift of the Atonement, a gift won through Christ's sacrifice and love.

We will probably never understand all we need to know about how to extend forgiveness, but perhaps these real-life stories, and others, can help us along the road. They have taught me that:

- Our own personal *desire* to forgive is critical.
- We can hold on to forgiveness as a goal, even while we are working toward it.
- Forgiveness is as much about our relationship

with the Lord as it is about our relationship with those who have wronged us.

- As we develop forgiving natures, we may refuse to be offended.
- We can forgive others for being who they are—and are not.
- Forgiveness sometimes requires a great deal of time, yet can happen in a moment.
- Forgiveness is a gift of the Atonement, a gift won through Christ's sacrifice and love.

Most motivating to me of all is the fact that forgiveness is sweet. It is indeed trading the spirit of heaviness for the garment of praise. How could the Lord be more generous to each of us? What is better than to lay down the burden of pain, to be healed by His love, and to then be free to extend that same love to those who have hurt us? That is truly the desire of my heart, and I intend to pray and work for it. I'm assuming you want to do the same.

Sources

Faust, James E. "The Healing Power of Forgiveness." *Ensign,* May 2007, 67–69.

Harper, James M., and Mark H. Butler. "Repentance, Forgiveness and Progression in Marriages and Families." In *Strengthening Our Families: An In-Depth Look at the Proclamation on the Family,* ed. David C. Dollahite. Salt Lake City: Deseret Book, 2000, 154–66.

Hinckley, Gordon B. "'Of You It Is Required to Forgive.'" *Ensign,* November 1980, 61–63.

Maxwell, Neal A. *Wherefore, Ye Must Press Forward.* Salt Lake City: Deseret Book, 1977.